AF209510

Malin Maria Hemberg

Life's unimagined potential

An inner space poetry of ease, awareness and love

© 2025 Malin Maria Hemberg

www.malinmaria.com

malinhemberg1@yahoo.com

Photo: Malin Maria Hemberg (Blomberg, Kinnekulle, Sweden)

Publisher: BoD · Books on Demand, Östermalmstorg 1, 114 42 Stockholm, Sweden, bod@bod.se

Printing: Libri Plureos GmbH, Friedensallee 273, 22763 Hamburg, Germany

ISBN: 978-91-8080-761-6

to my beloved son

give space within you
what is past is in the past, let it go
life is in the present
eternity exists only in love
the winner in love - always

PREFACE

Maria feels overwelmed. Was it a dream she just experinced? Where had the dream taken her? This morning in the middle of the living room floor, she feelt like she gained access to a new part of life. The candle flame flickering in the darkness and she could hear the icy wind howling outside the window. The blanket slid down from her shoulders and she stretched her legs in front of her to get the energy flowing in her body. The family is still sleeping, this time is her own.

The early morning was very special for Maria. She often got up early to meditate. The longing for breathing space had increased, as the need of inspiration, for the world to become bigger. The dreamlike state of the morning made anything seemed possible. She increasingly felt that everyday life had a less pleasant effect on her, as if it were holding her back and trying to limit her in many ways. It might be possible if you knew how, and if it felt good, but she felt she was just fumbling around in everyday life trying to support everyone until she no longer could. The pauses from life had become increasingly necessary. This was not how she wanted to live her life. She wanted more out of life, longed for genuine relationships and unconditional love. This morning she had closed her eyes, relaxed her mind through her breathing and drifted far away. She stepped into a new world and gained access to something that her life had been missing until now. A feeling she had never felt before or even known that she longed for.

Quietly she returns to the living room with the knowledge that something has happened within her. Something lasting. Something she will be able to return to. Over and over again. Eternally grateful and rich. Maria sits down in the armchair her grandmother once owned. A golden throne, she had imagined as a child. Now it was her favorite place. She lets the pen intuitively write down what she has just experienced, with the short lines flowing out of her.

Maria lowers her pen and takes a deep breath. Sees the written words in front of her. Reads the text aloud to herself in the flickering candlelight. Experiences everything a third time. She has opened a new door for herself this early morning. Everything is documented. She will come back here again and again. She has found the space of ease within herself. Finally, in this space anything can happen and it will.

Welcome to **Life's unimagined potential!**

SPACE OF EASE

a room of ease

early morning
everything is quiet
all doors are open
when do they close
seven o'clock
eight o'clock
nine o'clock
she will take the opportunity to visit
the different rooms
curiously explore
find out the code
to all the rooms
to be able to sneak in there
even during the day
when everyday life gets too busy
breath
to expand her consciousness
to expand in love
the everyday life mustn't diminish her

everyday life has that effect on her
to force her to rest
or adapt
or obey
or to be afraid
make it too simple for her
force her to fall into line
maybe it works for people
if they know where there are going
if it makes them feeling good
she rarely feels well
she rarely knows where she is going
she fumbles around in a shabby everyday life
until her feet no longer carry her
she stops seated
on exhibited benches
panting
the breaks becoming more frequent
until the whole head becomes one big break
the body a tired mass
the mind slow and terrified
this wasn't how she wanted to live
where did it go wrong
the early morning is hopeful
there´s she's clearly aware
of the different doors that surrounds her
in a quiet breath she lets her gaze sweep
from side to side
doors of different colors
she feels the carved wooden handle in her hand
they are made for each other

her hand and the wood
the faintly peach-colored door is scuffed
standing in front of this very door
the most worn out
the safest way
the one most used
she presses her hand down
realizes what scuffed means
that the door entices most
outside you can't see anything of its contents
nothing about its effect either
she lowers her expectations
decides to dare
the door is ajar
step in for a moment
begin something new
broaden one's consciousness
enrich everyday life
on the exhale she opens the door a little
the gap reduces
embrace the silence
she opens the door fully on the next exhale
takes a step in
to find herself in a thick mist
the oxygen-rich air is tangible
moistens her hair to curls
gets her sheer dress
closer to her skin
she stands still in the mist
before she slowly moves forward
into the unknown

step by step
let curiosity take over
the desire to understand uncertainty
the meaning behind her unconscious
embrace something, she doesn't understand
trust that the world she just entered
had not existed
if it hadn't meant anything
she let her thoughts run free
letting the oxygen-rich air fill her lungs
slowly
slowly
feels a bubbling in her nostrils
when she takes a breath
a conscious concentration
on what is
here and now
there's not much to hang onto in life
when the world is white
shifts her focus to her feet
feel the ground through her soles
decides to take off her shoes
to experience more
the soles of the feet receive a variety of sensations
about temperature
softness
hardness
stands still again
takes in what is
slowly starts moving
with small steps

the only compass she has is her inner one
what feels easy
what feels right
what meets resistance
she fills herself with confidence
curiosity and humility
can life be like this
easy
oxygen-rich
effervescent
being
she needs to feel this feeling within
inside her
it is there
within her
is it linked to location
or has the place only brought out the ability in her
once she has found it
will she be able to recreate it
in other contexts
she is grateful
something new has awakened within her
she has experienced something new
that she didn't know
that she longed for
slowly she takes another step
through and embraces of the white oxygen-rich mist
fills the lungs
pretending she's floating
smiling to herself
the thrill makes her feel relieved

it is the slowness
that creates focus in her life
when she consciously takes
one small step at a time
life will be
what her soul longs for
genuine
sincerely
not easier
but more simple
life develops
life has more feelings
slowness allows the choices to become clearer
when things go too fast
she doesn't see the possibilities
in the slowness there is time to have inner conversations
in the slowness everything has time to sink in
land in her own self
she feels genuine
she needs to be in tune with her soul
to achieve harmony in her relationships
to herself and others
she needs to stand with both feet firmly planted
when everything outside is spinning
she doesn't want to waste time
by driving too fast
and misses the important thing
or to drive into the ditch
she doesn't have time for that
life is too precious
life is now

always now
she needed this
the simple
nothingness makes her understand the greatness of life
what is important, for real
a walk quietly towards the door again
something has happened inside her
something that will always last
something she always wants to return to
the inner space of simplicity
over and over again
grateful and richer

a forest walk

she must get out
out into the forest
wander off the beaten paths
jump over streams
crawl under fences
lie down in the moss
treetops swaying in the wind
lying in the damp moss
her mind calms down
catches her breath
let's her eyes wander
branch to branch
tree to tree
clouds above the treetops
limitless
something is about to happen
everything points to that

she has no idea what
she doesn't want to hinder what's coming
she doesn't want to be a coward this time
she chooses to let everything happen

a door ajar

the stomach hurts
she almost loses her breath
she doesn't need
to bother anymore
she doesn't need
to compensate, prove and deny
there is nothing
to explain or defend
she can be
just as she is
as she is
with her faults and shortcomings
as she is
with her strengths
her strong integrity
as she is
with her strong desire
her unbridled creativity
as she is

with her sensitivity and intuition
she can be
just as she is
she can leave the door
ajar now
invite her friends to dinner
allow for care and love
smile at the world
let it return the smile
she can
she will
she shall
she remembers when she fantasized
played with the idea of being here
the idea was so easy
she literally floated
the heaviness within her died away
in her imagination she could feel free
that's when she understood
where she was going
now she was there
she lives her former longing
she floats with ease
it fills her outer and inner space
the warmth embraces her
the thrill of life grows within her

an emptiness creates space

emptiness comes as a reminder
it stops her
marvel the space
that's created within her
the space is open curiosity
she takes a breath
allows huge amounts of oxygen
fill her inner space
feeling like an internal massage
softens her inside
releases tension
increases circulation
she sees the effect
her reflection
the eyes are the mirror of the soul
hers sparkle again
joy has no best before date

space is what is needed
which is filled with simplicity
so simple

a free fall

she takes her dreams seriously
those who come to her at night
those who greet her during the day
they show a longing
a desire from deep within
they talk about what's important
not how
she is open to the how
her heart is open
she finds home in the wordless
that which cannot be explained
that which is undoubtedly tangible
completely uncompromising
she finds home in
that which makes her completely calm
and at the same time tickling her curiosity
in the complete safety
she finds the long-awaited simplicity
she realizes it was never either or

when she dares to express her innermost longing
throw herself recklessly
she is caught
she thought she was alone
it was just an illusion
she is held
in togetherness
she shares her reality
you can eat the cake
and save it
a reality she dreamed of
she is here now
the dream becomes reality

a thought let go

in the middle of her thought she lets it go
let it fly freely
it disappears immediately
from her memory
she looks around in wonder
what just happened
the feeling of sadness she had just felt
the one who got her
to collapse convulsively
disappeared in an instant
what was that thought she let out
she no longer remembers
then she realizes
if she could have remembered
she hadn't let it go completely
the joy of having the ability
to forget
spreads inside her
the sadness has left her

she breathes in easily
let's it spread into every void
feels it tickling her
she smiles at the feeling
she has been longing
so long
now her longing
is within her
ease fills the void

embracing ease

she has embraced ease
above all
defiantly consistent
in freedom flows life
the love
unconditional and generous
a conscious choice
a constant stream
she remembers
that freedom can be seen as threatening
freedom is so limitless
so uncertain
so unpredictable
in troubled times it is easy to believe
that restriction on freedom
is the solution
our world is symbiosis
if we isolate one
the other is affected

what we send out
we get in return
if you limit her
you increase your own limitations
if you give her freedom
you yourself will feel free
it's never you or her
it's always us
respect for every person
a matter of course
it changes everything
when we are being judged
we choose not to judge back
we don't need to
just noting the difference viewpoints
every viewpoint affects the feeling
different viewpoints can lead to disappointment
irritation and blame
perspective give birth to loving-kindness
peace and trust
this is every person's choice
so, what do we choose
the choice comes from within us
what's hidden deep in the heart
we must be true
to ourselves
towards our children
towards all the children of the future
we are all guides
we are constantly making new choices
we are the ones who create the future

an early spring

she accepts the inexplicable
finally, peace comes
she just needed to accept
that she doesn't have to accept
she just needs to understand
that she doesn't need to understand
she just needs to take responsibility
that she doesn't have to take responsibility for anyone else
she just needs to let go
the irritation softens and flows out of her
she fills the emptiness with fresh air
replaces the old and stale with the new and fresh
oxygen makes new seeds germinate
seeds she sowed long ago who were reluctant to grow
are now showing their growth potential
she is amazed
she just needs to accept
spring has arrived early this year
her former longing is now her reality

SPACE OF AWARENESS

a new frequency

there is a specific frequency
that touches her innermost being
it goes through time and space
through reality and imagination
it makes her calm and secure
inspired and hopeful
happy at the same time
completely loses her composure
she doesn't understand how it works
it wants her to expand the world
the inner and the outer
make it more
it provokes her
makes her insecure
take her out into new territory
the frequency has long been around the heart
attracted her
now increasing in strength
she doesn't know why but she listens and follows

a new way of living

she sits straight up from the bed
the light flickers from her movement
in the early hours
a feeling that she has
to go a long way in a short time
without a map or compass
she is swept away by the wind and the water
in the direction of the sun
every now and then
she lands on the earth
lies down on the ground
to still the dizziness
waiting for the next gust of wind or tidal wave
lets herself be swept away again
inhale a deep breath
sees the world ahead to collapse
like a house of cards
this wasn't how it was meant to be
the life

we need to learn again
what life is all about
start a new journey
far beyond our wildest imagination
after each new stage
we end up in a new reality
with new abilities
a deeper understanding
learn to feel comfortable more and more quickly
and gets bored just as quickly
thrown away again
the atrium of the new world
is the space of emptiness
the emptiness gives the time
to let go again
to know and understand
let go
previous needs
let go
previous roles
let go
previous longing for confirmation
we need to let go of everything
guided us
make us lose direction
towards the unconditional and infinite
reality tends to do otherwise
the spaces have the power
when they need to, they show up
abruptly out of nowhere
emotions are given free rein

in the uncertainty
when we lose what we think we need
it feels like we're losing our value
it is repeated
over and over again
that's why she practices
to embrace trust
in their intervals
embrace acceptance
in the void
she is reasoning internally
make new choices
disrupts old patterns
provides space for rest
takes care of herself
there are many methods
in her toolbox
space
time
warm
movement
flow
breathing
light
sound
ask for help
she becomes aware
about every little choice
reminds her
she is never alone
the key is unity

togetherness
there is no shortcut
to access the next reality
what it contains
she won't know
before she gets there
she just needs to get ready
she is like everyone else
nothing more
nothing less

our own process

we all have our own process
hers is to be open
lovingly true
she doesn't want to live
in some other way
she promised
to take oneself seriously
listen
be brave
she doesn't need to know
where things are leading
she moves towards
which gives life
longing
curiosity
which increases energy
she embraces
that and them
who gets her to like oneself

it helps her
to expand in love
respect her boundaries
listen to her yes
feel the longing of her soul
the energies in both directions
are extremely powerful right now
what she is drawn from
and what she is drawn towards

a beginning

suddenly she has gone all the way
to the goal she dreamt of
without understanding how it happened
luck
afterwards it feels obvious
the final destination had felt unattainable
a while ago
crazy
time-consuming
painful
suddenly she was here
she realizes that dream wasn't the goal
it's just a beginning
towards the next beginning

an internal responsibility

the feeling of sadness overwhelmed her
the first thought
you can never be truly happy
quickly replaced by
life's boundaries always exist
side by side
a constant choice
for everyone to make
the chosen thought affects the emotions
choice of path forward
what get the most space
which feeling should be priorities
she wants to take responsibility for everyone's happiness
she lets go of that thinking
the thought leaves a cavity
she must realize
that she doesn't have that ability
sadness washes over her
she has to let go

to avoid being drawn into the emotional states of others
it hurts to let go
in the void that is created
sorrow grows with plenty of space
the sorrow resonances loudly
she has difficulty staying focused
she must be her longing and desire
all starts with her
so she surrenders
let the sadness flow away
instead filled with gratitude
consideration and security
she lets it go
she cannot influence
side by side
there are extremes
her responsibility is her own inner self
it took a while to realize
now she knows
where she wants to be

an opportunity

when you start uncaring about
things you don't like
you instantly create
a lot of space
to fill
with things you love

one or more dimensions

she is learning to see everyday life
in as many dimensions as possible
why settle with one or a couple
what contrasts bring to life
she's having difficulty to polarize and judge
difficult to label things as right and wrong
all depends
her curiosity grows
humility too
when questions and answers are simplified
purpose and goals are easily lost
most people want all people living a good life
feel joy
meaningfulness
power of action
take responsibility for themselves
and each other
have we lost our way
who chosen the path

we are now slipping forward
who do we fool
why doesn't we stop
emergency signs flashing
along the way
we lose navigation
forced into applying the emergency brakes
sliding down the ditches
repeatedly
are we speed blind
do we need care
she chooses a forest path beside the highway
to feel the ground under her feet
to see the treetops
to jump over the stream.
to sit on a stump for a while
it's another dimension of reality
in nature everything is as it is
enormously complex
at the same time simple
life in symbiosis and diversity
she is unconditionally welcome
here
just as she is
the door is wide open
here
she is on her way
here
she is always here

a dream beyond doubt

she considers her dreams seriously
those who come to her at night
those who greet her during the day
they show a longing
a desire from deep within
they talk about what
not how
she is open for how
by opening the heart
for everything
everything that is here
here is her dream
beyond doubt

one board at a time

one board at a time
one by one
on the way
over water
under the sky
through the wind
slowly
viewing the horizon
for direction
let go of the future
turn your gaze towards the present
let every moment come alive
curiosity

a never-ending Lego build

she's like a constantly ongoing Lego build
smile at the feeling
constant processes are going on within her
there is no end
no end
no goal
over and over again
new creations are built up
different parts
creates new things
just to be then taken apart again
and create something new
it is a trial
an exploration and discovery
she has no idea
what is possible to create
next time
it's like after every completion
new pieces are added

as a reward
pieces that open
new opportunities
the construction takes place within her
life always happens on the inside
it is not possible to save old buildings
she needs to demolish
to create space
use the old pieces
to something new
when the old is dismantled
sadness sets in
fear and the emptiness
in the space she feels dizzy and faint
echoes and sways
she breathes deeper
moves slower
observes everything around her
when the dismantling is done
she sorts the parts
identifies the new arrivals
the feeling of curious tingling
the uncertainty of infinity
bit by bit
forming new wholes
some people build according to old drawings
trying to recreate the old
over and over again
they never get new pieces to their Lego builds
the desired security is replaced by boredom and bitterness
she sees it clearly know

her latest Lego build is demolished
she is in the void
along with uncertainty and self-doubt
she started sorting the pieces
her abilities and insights
she starts collecting the new ones that have been added
feel humility and gratitude
no idea how to use them yet
feeling a new spring on the way
a new structure
her interior is a constant Lego build
trust that everything is as it should be
she pours a glass of water
let her gaze wander outwards
through the window
nature is in a new phase
for construction
she is in a phase with nature
she is part of it

a huge dream

what thoughts is she repeating for herself
what memories does she carry with her
what does she spend her time doing
her thoughts and actions
constitutes her direction
no matter her desires
no matter her openness
hand to her heart
how ready is she
to change life
towards something better
she becomes her actions
she becomes her thoughts
is she inviting or uninviting
a moment with her own reflection
every day
simple questions
creates all the difference
is she who she wants to be

all change starts within her
what is she sending out to the surroundings
it's not a competition
if she doesn't make it one
everyone can be a winner
through the courage to dream huge
by putting into words longings
by sharing dream with the world
by joining hands with like-minded people
by separating the wheat from the chaff
without calculating
by making dreams come true
by letting the new reality
give birth to new, even bigger dreams

a way beyond

she takes another round in her thoughts
regarding truths
how we perceive reality
she sees different opinions
about how we perceive truths
and lies
is there one truth
is everything else lies
she doesn't want to use the word liar
there are different ways to look at reality
she wants to show respect
for other people's opinions
even while they are vastly different from hers
she wants the same respect back
to confirm someone's truth
as the only one existence
and give up one's own
does no good
she will never pretend to please someone else

no one owns someone else's truths
no one has a patent on perceiving reality
she will not fight
others can believe what they want about her
put her in a compartment
every person has that opportunity
to believe and perceive everything and everyone
just as they want
she is not participating in that war
it never ends
she has deviated from that path
the only truth that can be agreed upon
it's not possible to agree on a truth
there will always be different opinions
every human being has free will
every person is their own person
with their own free mind
she knows what she chooses
the perceptions bringing peace of mind
those that fill the body with warmth
those who give hope for the future
those who move her forward
she moves on
at her own pace

SPACE OF LOVE

an early dawn

she opened the door to infinite love
that overturns all beliefs
in her youth
didn't dare to go in
did not dare to accept
didn't dare to change
to throw herself out
thought it wasn't for her
she has always wanted to live life
in her own way
in small steps
regulated and secure
in a suit of shield
with action and knowledge
with understanding and well-trained abilities
the door is wide open now
she is still scared
but older
and aware

then she didn't understand her own fear
blamed everything outside of her
now she is aware of her fear
she will open the door
throw herself out
several centuries later
it's never too late
everyone always gets a second chance
balance is daring
spread the wings
surfing on the flowing source of life
she breathes deeply
totally ready
trusting life to carry her
for a long time, she thought
that she existed to enrich others
her purpose in life
realized finally that it wasn't true
she is here to be enriched
expand and develop
for her own good
researched and challenged
for her own good
for her own good
she is also able to help others
it's the effect
of taking oneself very seriously
realize that the hardest thing
is to understand one's own worth
everything she does
is for its own good

that means that no one
is indebted to her
everything she does is of her own free will
everything she says comes from her heart
everything is free
without expecting anything in return
that's why she won't need
to hold back
nice and scary
she is training
on thin ice

a release

the uncertainty was weaning
a faint whisper
everything is fine
all like it should be
she decided a long time ago
whatever happens
she needs to feel good
others may feel good
no one's well-being is above someone else's
no one's well-being should be at the expense of others
it is both a simple and complex thought
she also decided to let go
take responsibility for
the only thing she has power over
herself
her relationship with other people
everything else is beyond her
she wishes everyone the best
she refrains from judging

she can let go
show respect and trust
be at hand
if the need arises
let go
create space for the future
let go
make it impossible for the undesirable to continue
let go
cut the threads that feeds the destructiveness
reshape
innovate
still
thoughtfully
lovingly
nothing lasts forever
but eternity is always the goal
eternity carries lightness
love and the bright within
let us fill our insides with eternity
the only sustainable

a love connection

she wakes up early
slept restlessly
processed all the anxiety around her
it feels like she's been working all night
like a catalyst
a necessary job
a few deep breaths
she thinks about him
he who crossed her path in life
she lets the energy flow
throughout the body
long deep breaths
from top to toe
her body opens up immediately
she feels the lightness upwards
space in the heart
the thrill downwards
the stiffness is immediately replaced
with expansion
she almost loses her breath

the effect is tangible
how is it possible
a feeling of worry crosses her mind
a worry about being left alone
she thinks about the children
they are so beautiful
safe when they are with her
thinking about him again
the feeling through his energy is magical
the energy makes her love herself more
the energy makes her feel life-stirring and expansion
the energy makes her have faith in life and dare to dream
the energy makes her want to be herself fully
curious exploration
the energy makes her feel alive
the energy makes her become a better version of herself
makes her understand
the immense power of unconditional love
he helps her with all this
by its mere existence
she needs nothing more
everything happens beyond time and space
the energy is there
she exists
that's enough
she allows herself to be fulfilled
of an energy that is in abundance
she can share to everyone she meets
what she experiences
she doesn't want to hold back
it's not possible

the force is too great
she wants to spread
the unconditional love

an awakening

she wakes up to the aroma of coffee
beside the bed
and a whisper
do you want to go down to the beach
and see the sunrise
together with me
it feels like a dream
she doesn't want to wake up

a darkness contrasts the light

the darkness contrasts the light
she sees it so clearly now
when darkness took over
she undoubtedly saw the element of light
it called her loudly
it was time to go now
walk towards the light
against the warm it glows with
she didn't want to freeze anymore
she wanted to be embraced by the brightness
the darkness was the contrast she needed
it's easy to become blind in the dark
get lost
wander around in shadows
become dizzy and lost
without direction
believe in the light
it takes a small streak
to take a new direction

it requires trust
trust the wordless
aim the bright light through the darkness
in trust
life is like a dark midwinter's night
by moonlight
one of the very first
the pitch black darkness
then suddenly the sky bursts open
a crescent moon appears
a dim light
which the eyes can gratefully follow
one step ahead of the other
night after night the light increases
until the moon is full in its brightness
stars in the sky
snowflakes
spreads like a covering on the ground
helps illuminate the moonlight from below
she stands there in the middle of the night
feeling enlightened
embraced and held
the darkness is there
she smiles
she feels the light within her

the intention of a go-getter

what you do
is not the important thing
it's why
you do what you do
the intention
the creating touches her
acting out of anxiety and guilt
have no value for her
she is hopelessly ungrateful to that
she is sensitive
like a child
a child feels a parent's intention
the child fills up with warmth or
feelings of guilt create distance
it's easy to get carried away
easy to lose each other
in the everyday doing
so easy to forget
to be lovingly present
so easy to forget

that one's own meaning is more important
than a disassembled dishwasher
so easy to belittle
a moment of eye contact
a hug means more
than the shoes standing in line
it is not what you do that matters
that's why you do what you do
the intention
in your actions that affect her
she wants to meet you
make sure you understand
that you are important just as you are
she knows how you feel
beyond everything you do
gifts and services must come
from a loving place
otherwise it has little value
for her

a choice

she sinks down
in the warm water
creates a gap in everyday life
opportunities appear
she seizes the opportunities
make them yours
the water gives her peace
creates space for new ideas
in space everything is
she has been holding back
here can she feel unconditional love for everything
all is okay
a new feeling
to be able to connect on someone's energy
experience expansion to explosion
can you do that
must one ask permission
can you do it secretly

is it noticeable
can you ask such questions
who can answer
she believes that one can
the energy she has connected to
makes everything so easy
she gets access to the simple
the playful life
she feels the smile on her lips
feel the sparkle in her eyes
life is messing with her
what has been outside her consciousness
has found the way into her
taken place
so much space she transforms
like a bearded father
she decides that you can connect
because nothing can be owned
this consciousness belongs to all
everything is divisible
everyone is one and the same
meant to help each other
make each other grow
she has connected herself
on a frequency
which is so much bigger than she imagined
she is floating
getting dizzy
losing breath
she doesn't want to be anywhere else
feels that everything is within her

she is charging her batteries
as long as she needs
eternally grateful
for the opportunity
who came to her now
she flows forward
the breath is undulating
attention is razor sharp
differentiating ability is brutal
her intention is endless love
can you opt out of the conditional
just the idea of conditioning love and care
makes her suddenly want to vomit
she has no choice anymore

an irresistible love energy

when she thinks about her friend
she is filled with a overwhelming loving feeling
she can barely accommodate it
it leaks out through her
her inner critic wonders
if it is an escape
a fantasy
maybe even a mania
it can't be real
the other voice assures her
that it is the great power of unconditional love
the one who can move mountains
create peace
order chaos
the one who asks for nothing
never gets suffocating
or too much
it transforms
lifts up

it is powerfully tangible
maybe unaccustomed
in a good and necessary way
the power the world needs now
the one we need to share with each other
stretch out your hands
hook arm
form a pearl necklace over the earth
she collects pearls
she sees many shining
like stars in the night sky
her conviction is strong
her soul knows
it speaks to her
it is too clear
this is bigger than she dares to understand
she lets go of understanding
trust in the path she is now walking
the one who loves the most wins
the name of the book she is now reading
it shows the path she has taken
her heart is beating fast
she realizes it's time for the next step
whether she dares or not

a true love

she lets herself be embraced by him
his gaze is warm and loving
don't apologize for who you are
our needs and feelings are not intertwined
they can stand up for themselves
they are not dependent on each other
we like to believe that
but that's not true
he is looking for words
to explain what she needs to hear
what they both need to hear
he looks her deep in the eyes
I am afraid of losing you
but it's not your responsibility
to make me feel safe
it's not you who creates the insecurity
it is within me
it's not my responsibility either
that you will feel free

it's not me who makes you unfree
that feeling is inside you
I love all of you
the whole creative and independent person you are
it is you
I don't want to make you compromise on that
for my needs
it would give me guilt and a bad conscience
what you are would disappear
I would get less from you to love
in the same way that it's not your job
to keep me safe at all times
it would be a false sense of security
which would constantly need to be replenished
she listens attentively to him
it's so easy to get lost
in their desire to do good and help
so easy to go wrong
belittle both oneself and others
to act directly
on the ugly that appears
instead of receiving the feeling
investigate it
gratefully accept it
don't be afraid
it's just a feeling
not a truth
I need to replace the fear of losing you
in gratitude that you are now there
in my life
no matter what happens

have you been here
you have awakened something within me
something I will always treat
as the most beautiful gift
he takes her hands
press them gently
you must be able to express yourself
in the ways that are you
to soar high above the trees
now and then
where you get your energy
gain perspective
you are not a swan
who is happy with a pond
you are many birds
in one and the same
a part of you
is a faithful swan
you create complete presence
total attention to the person you meet
but you have to get up and fly
to take stock of life
I love that ability
you have to be yourself
all parts
nothing is easy
neither to adapt
or to be your whole self
but will humanity survive
and flourish
there is only one way

I wonder if anyone knows
how to become purposeful
when you have something you can become really good at
and longing for
I see it in you too
you want to change the world through you
he then lets the silence speak for a while
the calm embraces
she takes in what he has just said
the walls around them are falling
like a house of cards
the whole world becomes visible
around them
everything is happening now
it is for real
she embarrasses the magic
let it transform
her whole being feels blessed and carried

a light hand on the cheek

you are sufficient
let the clenched hand relax
instead, lightly stroke it across your cheek
stretch out both arms
let in the love that wishes you well

she is sufficient
she lets the clenched hand relax
instead, lightly stroke it across the cheek
she chooses to stretch out both arms
she lets in the love that wishes her well

he is sufficient
he lets the clenched hand relax
instead, lightly stroke it across the cheek
he chooses to stretch out both arms
he lets in the love that wishes him well

I am sufficient
I let the clenched hand relax
instead, lightly stroke it across your cheek
I choose to stretch out both arms
I let in the love that wishes me well
so the world changes

an unconditional love relationship

leave the window ajar
let the oxygen-rich air in
everything is quiet
breathing getting slower and slower
she remembers the end
which opened up for a new beginning
how they chose each other
she and he
she
she wanted to feel loved and free
she calmed down
went inward
listened
peeled off
got to know herself
the feeling was inside her
she has to make herself happy
become her own best friend
responsive and generous

when she learned that
new opportunities opened up
he
he wanted to feel loved and free
he calmed down
went inward
listened
peeled off
bravely stepped out
everything was within him

the new day dawns
she wakes up early
she crawls close
lies still
hold him for a long time
slowly they both wake up
she meets his eyes
with a clearer gaze than ever
gently and sympathetically he gives
her a new experience of pleasure
so beautiful that tears flow
along her cheeks
she feels completely safe
in his presence
he does everything through unconditional love
he feels for her
the boundaries between them are blurred
their bodies unite
in complete harmony
they change rhythm

the closeness and warmth make her ache with happiness
a relief that comes when the resistance disappears
she feels taken by surprise
where have you been
she whispers to him in a soft voice
she has longed for him so much
longed so much for their we
when their past cracked
they were drawn to each other like magnets
there was no longer anything
that kept them apart
in vulnerability lies power
who embraced the other's soul
when everything falls
can love flow freely
when love flows freely
they are home again
she is getting to know herself again
every day
over and over again
leaves who she was
embracing a new version of herself
he does the same
get to know himself again
leaves who he was
embracing a new version of himself
they have taken their backpacks off
they meet in their nakedness
vulnerable and humble
brave and confident
autumn is approaching

what has been grown can be harvested
nothing is taken for granted
everything is a blank slate
that's how it has to be
the innermost essence of love
she has to make herself happy
become her own best friend
responsive and generous
when she learned that
she could love more
he must make himself happy
become his own best friend
responsive and generous.
when he learned that
he loved more
there's a familiar tingling inside her now
she takes an extra long breath
to provide adequate space
the air is both light and tough at the same time
she registers every occurrence within herself
with a sensitivity that surprises her
the vibrations spread from the inside out
they are liberating and vibrant
she just needs to breathe
let it happen
close her eyes for a short while
feel the neck
on the back of the head
up towards the temples
she feels under the sole of her foot
lowest on the fingertips

it's like inner caresses under the skin
in the bloodstream
she let it happen
in the early morning
the night has peeled off all its layers
she starts from the beginning again
all that matters is

a firework of love

a short break
her gaze is fixed
a bit ahead
unclear what
a few deep breaths
life's extremes are mixed
over and over again
she is everything at the same time
sadness and joy
lightness and resistance
simplicity and complexity
a lot of everything
in a mess
a moment to stop the spinning
sort out the mess
the space she creates is important
she wants to face everything
with presence and courage
therefore she lets go of what has been

breathe in what is
sorts and prioritizes
focus on the future
it's ringing next to her
she twitches
the immediate concern
an old memory that is triggered
the anxiety disappears quickly
she has been working on herself
her concern
she is well aware
that the reaction no longer serves any function
it's part of her story now
the threat no longer exists
instead a smile spreads across her face
she relaxes
the words to her are a firework of love
written with care and appreciation
the heart takes a leap
there someone who knows her better than she does herself
she doesn't need to explain longer
just accept
what she is experiencing now
she treats everyone
to become enriched
lifted up with complete trust and acceptance
safe and loving
with open doors
to life's unimagined potential
the pinging is now a reminder
I am here for you.

I love you unconditionally
because you are you

a loving home

she sits up in bed with a jerk
wide awake
the heart must beat twice after such an awakening
but she is very calm
finally
as she has longed for to suffice in every way
for everything
for everyone
she is enough
the feeling she has lived with for a long time
has completely ceased
others are allowed to think and feel as they wish
want more and less
but she is enough
she leaves the rest there
she moves on
towards the next level
next time in life
it's like her current life

contains many lifetimes
in one and the same
experiences and lessons learned are allowed to sink in
open up to new opportunities
some things are constant
others are completely changed
it's a new time now
everything will deepen
become more powerful
warmer
more loving
she will not be held back
or limited
it's real now
she is enough
for everything and everyone
just as she is
the time of inadequacy is finally over
everything is as it should be
she breathes in the early morning
the light flickers on the windowsill
she hears the wind outside
summer has taken a break
just like her
the aroma of coffee reaches her
the bed is soft
may her interval be quiet
simultaneously intensively
she turned inside out on herself
in the daylight
seen both in the exterior

and the inner luggage
it is the function and the energy
that determines the future
is it time to say goodbye or to hook the arm forward
does it give her a push or does it slow down
she does not value
value easily creates guilt and shame
she notes
accepts with gratitude and love
everything is what they are
time has its course
she wants to continue
don't brake
don't rush
keep pace
with life
breathes through its lungs
one breath at a time
as if every breath
would be the most precious gift
the most beautiful smile
the most beautiful caress
that makes every cell tickle her abode in the gap
does she have time to feel all this
in the room of ease
now she is returning home
home to the loving
from this place she can be curious
back to life
it's time to continue exploring
playfully try

respectfully balance
there is no conclusion
everything is as it should be
one step at a time
first, she will drink coffee

Thanks

for support and help

Tea

Martin

a new challenge and uncharted territory

to try to reformulate the words in a new context

first time is the first time

next time can never be the first time

my world is bigger now

Malin Maria